101 Questions for Men

Coffee Table Philosophy

Book II

J Edward Neill

Cover Graphic by J Edward Neill

Tessera Guild Publishing

 Téssera

ISBN- 13: 978-1511434270
ISBN- 10: 1511434279

For armchair philosophers everywhere.

What is life, if not a question with infinite answers?

Beginner's Luck

If you could be the last man alive in a world fully populated with women, would you?

Fill in the Blank

The truest measure of a man's worth is _____.

Ask Dick Cheney

When is war the answer?

Along the Same Lines

If you were the general of an army conducting an *absolutely necessary* war, would you:

A. Destroy the enemy by any means? No matter the collateral damage?

B. Engage the enemy *only* when civilians are unlikely to be injured or killed?

C. Use a nuclear weapon with the hope that a singular show of force would prevent a prolonged conflict?

If you don't have Kids, Pretend

If you could only teach your child two lessons in life, what would the lessons be?

Ask the Ladies to leave the Room

Be utterly honest.

Whenever you meet an attractive woman for the very first time,

what is your first and most instinctive thought?

That thing Thomas Jefferson said

Are all men truly created equal?

If so, are they equal despite physical and intellectual differences?

If not, name the characteristics causing them to be *less* than equal.

The Top Three things you'd be Willing to Fist Fight over are:

_____

_____

_____

The Little Blue Button

Suppose you had a blue button in front of you.

And suppose pressing this button would make every other human

in the world instantly and painlessly assume your belief system

(whatever it may be.)

Would you press it?

Shallow End of the Pool

Which woman would you prefer:

A.   Stunningly beautiful, yet profoundly unintelligent?

B.   Sweet and intellectually gifted, yet badly scarred and
wheelchair-bound?

Judge, Jury, Executioner

Define what your punishment would be for each of the following crimes. Assume each was perpetrated with malicious intent:

Theft

Assault

Murder

Rape

Child Abuse

Culture Mulch

Assume there is such a thing as a *typical* family household.

Are there certain tasks men should *always* perform?

What about women?

Interstellar

Suppose the world will end in ten years. From today until that time, everything on Earth will be normal. But once the tenth year rolls around, all life will end instantly.

You can save your family by flying alone to a distant planet and terraforming it.

You'd have to leave tomorrow, and you'd never see them again.

Will you get on that spaceship?

Finish this Sentence

The primary force behind the way I live my life is:

A. Survival

B. Search for knowledge

C. Spiritual growth

D. Wealth

E. Sex

F. _____?

There and Back and There Again

You've been given a time machine.

It will work three times before it breaks.

When and where are you going?

Do you use the final time to return to your present life?

Ghost in the Machine

Suppose that when you die, you earn the choice to become either a
guardian angel *or* a malevolent spirit.

You can either protect one single person for their entire life.

Or haunt someone and ruin all their endeavors (good or bad.)

Which would you choose?

Whom will you protect or haunt?

Politics

Worthy of everyone's time, passion, and best mudslinging skills?

A horrid profession performed by highly questionable people?

Or something to be approached with great caution, and only by the very wisest of us?

Unstoppable Force, Immovable Object

Choose which *one* you'd prefer to be:

Impossibly fast and agile

Incredibly, inhumanly strong

Extremely charismatic

Absurdly intelligent

Explain why.

True or False?

Is the best *defense* a strong *offense*?

War of Words

Picture yourself having a colorful, perhaps even vicious argument with a woman. In this particular argument, you happen to be 100% right.

Is it better to continue the battle and prove your point?

Or to give up your position and make peace?

Now picture the same situation, but with a male friend.

Professional Athletes

Supremely fun to watch? Worth every penny they earn?

Arrogant? Overpaid? Overhyped?

Fun to watch, but otherwise Neanderthal-ish?

As nuanced a group of people as any other segment of society?

Best of Both Worlds

Choose which life you'd prefer:

A.   A happy marriage to a beautiful woman. With happy children. And a thriving social life.

B.   Extreme success in a field of your choosing, earning you excellent financial rewards, global recognition, and a high level of personal freedom.

Let's Play Limbo.

Assume you're in an exclusive romantic relationship.

Name the ideal number of times per year you'd like to have sex.

Now name the absolute minimum.

If the number dropped below the minimum, how low would it have

to go before you'd consider having an affair?

The Front Lines

If a foreign country invaded your home nation tomorrow, would
you immediately take up arms and rush to the fight?
Assume you have children of fighting age. Would you let them
join you?
Also assume you are married. Would you resist if your wife
wanted to fight beside you?

Fight Club Time Machine

Suppose you're given the chance to travel back in time to fight any one historical figure to the death.

If you defeat them, the course of history will be changed in accordance with their absence.

The fight will be hand-to-hand. Your foe will be in their prime.

Whom will you fight?

The Latest Google Device

Imagine you've been given a special optic lens which allows you
to see women's thoughts whenever and wherever you like.
However, whenever you wear it, they'll be able to see *your*
thoughts as well.
Would you wear it?
What if only 10% of your thoughts were visible?

Priorities

Given your life and all the routines therein, what percentage of
your existence is meaningful?

Satisfying?

Wasteful?

Human Piñata

As punishment for a crime you've committed, you are to be
inflicted with one of the following conditions. The court mandates
this condition will last your entire life. Choose your punishment:

Extreme physical weakness

The loss of 25 IQ points

The loss of your left hand

A permanent 80 lb. weight gain

Wormhole

If scientists opened a stable wormhole that could take you to any point in the universe via spacecraft, and if you were given a round-trip ticket to use this wormhole to visit the location of your choice, where would you go?

Explain your choice.

A Terrible Power

Pretend you've been given a weapon of immense power.

If you use it, it will wipe out any one single nation on earth, and then vanish forever.

If you don't use it, you must pass it along to another person.

Would you use it?

If so, on what nation?

If not, whom would you pass the weapon to?

Chameleon

Name three things you would willingly allow a woman to change about you in order to better your relationship with her.

If you can't name three, (or any) explain.

Nightmare Scenario

Name one thing that truly, utterly terrifies you.

Explain why.

Who needs Helmets?

Pretend you're a world-class athlete.

You've secured a five-year contract worth $500 million dollars

playing a sport you love.

At the end of the contract, you will retire.

But you'll play knowing there's a 100% chance you'll suffer at

least one highly damaging injury during your career.

Will you sign the contract?

Tools of the Trade

In terms in war, is it less than honorable to kill your enemies using missiles and bombs?

Is fighting with guns less honorable than with swords?

Is honor relevant in war?

Fact or Fiction

Is truth best defined as:

A. What can be *proven* using the best modern scientific method?

B. What is universally *perceived* to be real? (I.e.; if *everyone* believes in a thing, does reality matter?)

C. An individual's experience of the world. (I.e.; if you see a *red* apple but I see the same apple as being *green*, what color is the apple really?)

Judgment Day

Approximate the value of your life's actions.

Assign a percentage value to your good deeds and another value to your bad deeds. The total must equal 100%.

For example, in terms of what you've done with your life, perhaps 97% has been good and only 3% bad.

Pretend that if your bad deeds exceed 5%, you'll be sent to Hell.

Feeling warm yet?

The Ultimate 'What if?'

If you could be a woman for one single day, would you?

Assume no one but you will ever know.

If yes, what would you like to experience?

What age would you want to be?

What situation would you want to be in?

If no, why not?

Survivor: Couch Edition

This is a question suited for larger groups.

Look around you. Consider everyone else in the room with you.

If global apocalypse struck tomorrow, who would survive the

longest?

Why?

Kneel before Zod

Religion and gods aside, is there anything in the world worthy of worship?

Cosmic Thunderbolt

Given the choice, how would you prefer to die?

We Come in Peace (or not)

Imagine you are earth's emissary to a strange, faraway planet.
Upon landing your spaceship, you immediately encounter what
appears to be friendly alien life.
What are the first three things you say to them?

Apples and Trees

Fill in the blanks. One word each.

The three best virtues a father can possess are:

_____

_____

_____

Do you possess any of these?

The Coldest Shoulder

In terms of emotional treatment, what is the cruelest thing a man could say or do to his wife or lover?

The Recluse

Could you live alone, *no outside contact at all*, and be happy?
If not, why?

Fight or Flight

Is a man a coward if he:

Backs down from a fist fight with a larger man?

Evades conscription into the army?

Commits suicide?

Strikes a woman in self-defense?

Cries due to being made fun of?

Hammer of Injustice

Imagine you've been placed on Death Row for a crime you didn't commit.

Your execution is in 60 seconds.

What are your last words?

A Storm is Coming

A horrific tornado is moments away from hitting your house. Your
underground storm shelter is only big enough to fit 3 people.
You live with your wife, your child, your mother, and your father.
You have the only storm shelter key.
Who's in?
Who's out?

First Impressions

Do you ever predict a woman's behavior based on her mode of dress?

In other words, if she's dressed revealingly, do you assume anything about her?

What if her style is demure?

Remember…no Takebacks

Pretend you're writing the woman of your dreams a sincere love letter.

The content of this letter will decide whether or not she comes to visit you or stays right where she is.

What does the *last* sentence in your letter say?

Funny, the Dog Never Seemed to Mind

For $1,000,000, would you agree to never have sex again?

For $10,000,000

For $500,000?

Cream of the Crap

The three *worst* attributes of humanity are:

_____

_____

_____

In One Word

What is the most beautiful thing in the known universe?

A Simpler Life

Imagine a red switch.

If you turn this switch, *all* modern technology (vehicles, computers, television, machines, weaponry, etc.) will vanish from the world.

Everyone's lives will return to a pre-industrialized state.

With one exception: modern medicine will remain intact.

You hittin' the switch?

Nostradamus

Given what you know about the way the world is progressing, what do you predict for the state of humanity in 100 years? Describe your predicted future in detail.

Patience

For many years, you've been madly in love with a beautiful,
successful, intelligent woman.

Only trouble is, she's married with a young child.

She says she'll be with you as soon as the child turns nineteen.

Will you wait for her?

Will you pressure her for an affair?

Or will you move on?

Happy Birthday, Mr. President

Imagine you have the chance to be elected the ruler of whatever nation you live in.

Would you accept the position?

If so, what is your first act once you're in office?

Frienemies

Suppose you've endured a tough divorce with a woman you once
loved.
You have two kids together.
She's getting remarried.
Can you imagine any scenario in which you and her new husband
become best friends?

It's Friday Night

Loud, raucous party with thirty fun strangers?

Laid-back evening at a quiet establishment with two good friends?

Sitting on a starlit beach with a pretty girl?

Alone and untroubled in the most peaceful place imaginable?

This is the End

The world will end tomorrow.

You have exactly 24 hours to live.

You have the resources and access to do anything you want until

the end comes.

How do you spend your 24?

Not this time, Pal

Name three instances in which you would *not* risk your life to save another human being.

Mirror, Mirror, on the Wall

If someone were to tell you they love *themselves* as much as they
love others, would you assume they were shallow?

Narcissistic?

Or in possession of a healthy sense of self-worth?

What if they said they loved themselves *more* than they love

anyone else?

Sacrifices

Would you give your life to:

Save all the babies in an infants' nursery?

Rescue all the residents of a retirement home?

Save a hospital ward populated with terminally ill people?

Protect an apartment complex occupied by homeless?

Save an entire prison colony?

Have Fun

Define the meaning of Time.

Buckets

Name three things you believe every man should do before he dies.

Seriously, go find a Pen

Fill in the blanks with three things that utterly repulse you:

_____

_____

_____

Swimming in the Deep End

Do you believe the universe exists for the purpose of sustaining
life?

Suppose the laws of nature were different. Do you believe *no* life
would exist?

Or would life simply be different?

Explain.

Not Knowing is Half the Battle

Name three situations in which ignorance is bliss.

Ever Seen The Neverending Story?

Take a deep breath.

Close your eyes.

Put down your beer.

Now do your best to describe the concept of *nothing*.

Maybe we're just 1's and 0's

Imagine that the universe and everything in it are illusions. As in humans, animals, planets, and stars…all artificial.

Now imagine this illusion is governed by super-intelligent beings who are above and beyond our awareness.

Describe what you think these beings might look like.

What's their purpose?

How long will they keep playing the game?

In the Shadows

Is it possible that such fears as the Bogeyman, The Monster Under
the Bed, and night terrors come from primal memories of
something real?
In other words, ten thousand generations ago, did monsters exist?
Or are these terrifying thoughts our minds' way of giving
substance to our subconscious?

Portals

Pretend that scientists have perfected the creation of teleportation devices.

These devices are capable of instantaneously transporting one single person from one location to another.

You've been given two portals. One leads to the other, and vice versa.

Where would you put your two portals?

Small Potatoes

If tomorrow you learned that awareness ends at death, no afterlife exists, and that human life has no greater meaning, would you be:

Extremely sad?

Relieved?

In a state of disbelief?

Unaffected?

_____?

A World Full of Homer Simpsons

Imagine you could have yourself cloned multiple times.
Your clone will be just like you, only it will do *everything* you tell
it to do: *your job, your chores, your romantic responsibilities, etc.*
However, each copy you make reduces your intelligence by 5%.
How many times would you hit the 'copy' button?

Villains Point-of-View

If, in order to have any chance at happiness, you had to commit yourself to doing evil or immoral deeds on a regular basis, would you?

With Sugar on Top

What is mankind's greatest achievement?

What about yours?

You Mad, Bro?

Think of your worst rival. Perhaps this person is your outright enemy, or perhaps someone you simply have disdain for. In any event, you don't like them.

Name three redeeming qualities they possess.

Triple Dog Dare

This one is for parties or gatherings of more than one person.

Tell the person nearest to you one thing no one else knows about you.

Lions, Tigers, and Dragons

Is man the most dangerous animal?

I'll wait for the Movie

Pretend two books sit before you.

In one, the secrets of the universe all the way back to the beginning

are revealed.

If you read the other book, you'll be happy for the rest of your life.

You can only read one of the two.

Which book will you take?

The Short List

Name four things you *wouldn't* do in exchange for
$1,000,000,000.

Unlucky 7's

It's sometimes said there are seven deadly sins:

Greed, Pride, Gluttony, Lust, Sloth, Wrath, and Envy

Which one is the worst?

Which one are you most guilty of?

Just don't *Forget*

Think hard.

Is there any such thing as a truly unforgivable act?

For example, if someone did something truly despicable, but spent the rest of their life doing good deeds to atone for it, would they be worthy of your forgiveness?

Lighten the Mood a Little

In terms of sports and games, which one represents the purest form
of human athletic prowess?

Examples: soccer, American football, basketball, *golf*, etc.)

In the Sand. With a Stick

Draw the line between confidence and arrogance.

Where is it?

Apologies to the Lonely

Think of a woman you've dated, married, or otherwise enjoyed the
romantic company of.
Given her personality, if she had been a man, would you still have
befriended her?
If not, why?

Not Everyone's a Giver

Is searching for one's own happiness a noble quest?

Is it ordinary and to be expected of a human?

Can it be described as selfish?

Wasn't Fishing Season Anyway

It's sometimes said that if you love someone, let them go. In romantic terms, assuming it were for her benefit, would you ever *willingly* let go of a woman you loved?

Reality TV

Imagine you're going to be stuck on a desert island for one year.
You get to pick one book, one piece of music, and one person to be
stuck on the island with you.

Name your picks.

If everyone you knew were going to be in the same situation,
would any of them pick *you*?

Mad Men

Imagine you have the power to reverse modern culture to where it was approximately 70 years ago.

As a man, you'll have access to all the privileges of existing in a pre-feminist world.

Considering all the implications, would you hit reverse or continue to live in modern culture?

Throw Money at the Enemy

In the modern era, the United States government has allocated as much as 21.9% and as little as 16.0% of its annual budget for the Department of Defense.

The total yearly expenditure rose from $266 billion in 1996 to as much as $721 billion in 2010.

Given the choice, what percentage would you spend?

451

Are there *any* books, art, music, or movies you would ban?

For everyone?

For children only?

If they were sufficiently subversive or distasteful, would you ever order these works destroyed?

Objectively Speaking

Consider a person, a group of people, or even an entire nation that
you might view as a rival or an enemy.
Do you believe it's possible these individuals want the same things
in life as you?
Or are they fundamentally wrong in how they choose to live?

The Straightest Line Imaginable

In terms of gaining *your* full romantic attention, what's the fastest
way a woman could succeed in doing so?

What about men in general? What's the fastest way to their hearts?

Is it better to...

A.   Wear your heart on your sleeve?

B.   Be cautiously optimistic?

C.   Be well-guarded, but allow situationally appropriate emotions to escape?

D.   Be a stone wall. Strong and unbreakable.

Dating Cleopatra

Suppose you could bring any woman from history back to life in order to date her. Or even just to be friends.

Got anyone in mind?

Xbox and Beer

Accounting for all 24 hours, describe how a perfect day would go for you.

Keep Quiet, or Else

It has been said that, *"Those who trumpet their suffering are often most deserving."*

Meaning that people who complain or otherwise announce their troubles might deserve whatever inflicts them.

True or false?

The Omega Project

Imagine you've been elected to lead all of humanity.

Your goal: bring every living human together for the purpose of completing a singular, grand project.

The project can be anything imaginable, so long as it's scientifically plausible.

What will you lead humanity to do?

Exile

Suppose you could utterly annihilate any *one* thing in the entire world.

It could be a person, place, idea, behavior, or object.

What would you exile?

The Glue that Binds

Is it possible most societies across the world are held together by
an unspoken threat of violence?

In other words, is the fear of imprisonment, retribution, and death
the real reason polite civilizations are able to exist?

Or is there another, most powerful reason?

And Be Careful What You Wish For

If you could ask all the women in the world one question and have them answer completely and truthfully, what would it be?

Thank you for reading.

This entry in the Coffee Table Philosophy series felt obvious to me.

Refining my questions to 49% of the world's population was a challenge I looked forward to.

I saw at it as a way of compiling conversations had by guys (and probably girls, too) at every tavern, ballgame, and barbeque.

Because I believe the surest way for man to increase his knowledge is to ask questions.

And I believe that rather than *telling* the world his answers…

…his best course of action is to *live* them.

About the author

J Edward Neill became obsessed with writing in early 2001. On one bitterly cold morning in the lowest corridor of his candlelit man-cave, he fingers to keyboard and began hammering away on what would soon become a lifelong obsession. Since that day, he has spent nearly all his free time lost in his daydreams, conjuring ways to write the kind of stories he loved as a child.

When he's not glooming in front of his laptop or iPad, J Edward haunts the internet via his websites: *www.TesseraGuild.com* and *www.DowntheDarkPath.com*. He currently lives in the North Georgia 'burbs, where he moonlights as a foodie, a sipper of too much pinot noir, and the hugest-armed quarterback never to sniff the NFL.

101 Questions for Men is his second non-fiction book.

Also available by J Edward Neill

Non-Fiction

101 Questions for Humanity – Coffee Table Philosophy Part I

Novels

Down the Dark Path – Book I in the Tyrants of the Dead trilogy

Dark Moon Daughter – Book II in the Tyrants of the Dead trilogy

Hollow Empire – Night of Knives (a serial novel co-authored with

John Mcguire)

Short Stories

Old Man of Tessera

The Sleepers

And coming soon…

Nether Kingdom – Book III, the chilling conclusion to the Tyrants of the Dead series

Let the Bodies – A sequel to the horror short, Old Man of Tessera

Darkness Between the Stars – Prequel to the Tyrants of the Dead trilogy

101 Questions for Women – Coffee Table Philosophy Part III

6894543R00067

Printed in Germany
by Amazon Distribution
GmbH, Leipzig